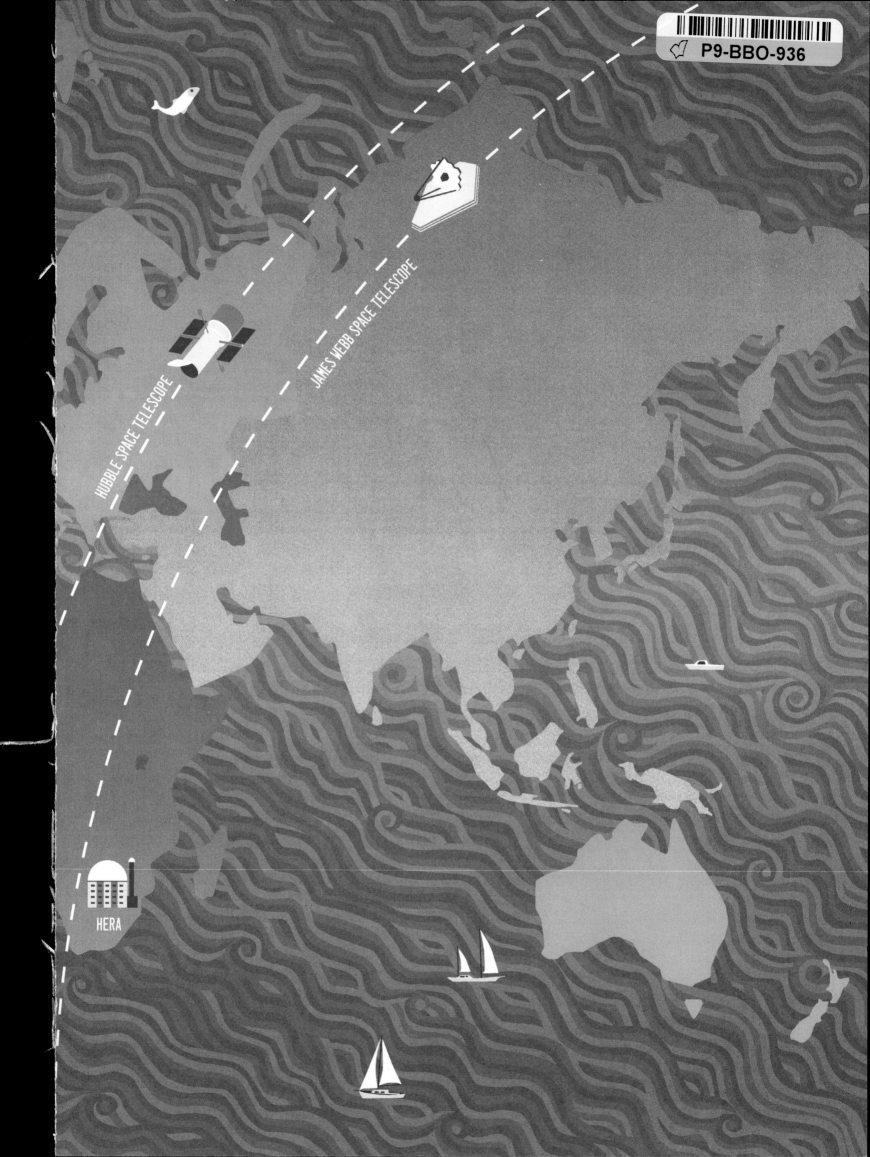

HUBBLE SPACE TELESCOPE

JAMES WEBB SPACE TELESCOPE

HERA

Jacob would like to thank Rich Matsuda, Carlos Alvarez and the staff of the Keck Observatory for sharing their expertise, Stephanie Scholz for opening his eyes to the beauty of telescopes, and his editors at Flying Eye. In researching this book, Jacob drew information and inspiration from *Eyes on the Sky: A Spectrum of Telescope* by Sir Francis Graham-Smith, which he highly recommends.

To my great loves, Ari and Fred
- Stephanie Scholz

First American edition published in 2021 by Flying Eye Books,
an imprint of Nobrow Ltd. 27 Westgate Street, London E8 3RL.

Text © Jacob Kramer 2020
Illustrations © Stephanie Scholz 2020

Every attempt has been made to ensure any statements written as fact have been checked to the best of our abilities. However, we are still human, thankfully, and occasionally little mistakes may crop up. Should you spot any errors, please email info@nobrow.net.

1 3 5 7 9 10 8 6 4 2

Printed in Poland on FSC® certified paper.

ISBN: 978-1-912497-68-3

www.flyingeyebooks.com

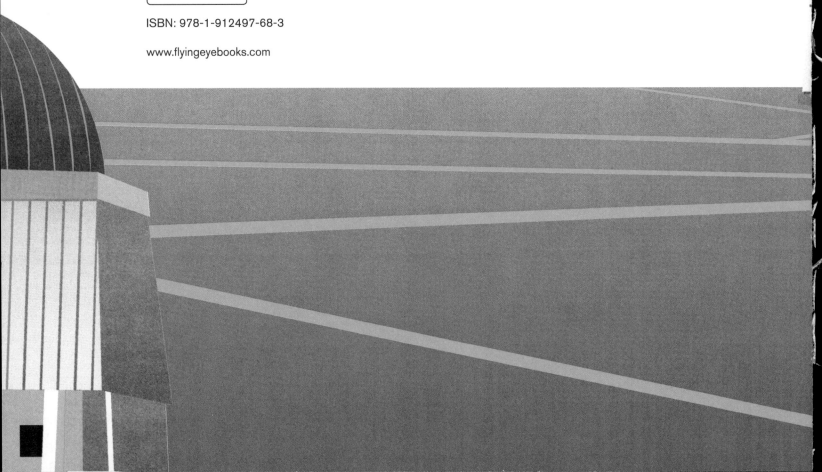

LOOKING UP

JACOB KRAMER & STEPHANIE SCHOLZ

FLYING EYE BOOKS
LONDON | NEW YORK

CONTENTS

LOOKING UP

For hundreds of thousands of years, people have looked into the sky and seen lights. During the day they saw the Sun and sometimes the Moon. At night, they saw stars and planets twinkling in the sky.

They wondered:

"What are these lights?"
"Why do they move?"
"Where do they go?"

"Are they gods?"
"Are they hungry?"
"What do they like to eat?"

All over the world, people kept records of where each star appeared in different seasons. They named the stars and grouped them into shapes called constellations. Using calendars, each group of people tried to answer the questions, but they only had their own eyes to look with.

SIGHT

Most animals have eyes, which they use to look at things.
Some people can see different colors, other people can't. Some
animals, like bees and snakes, can see light that is invisible to us.

Telescopes are like large eyes. We build
them in quiet, dark places to see far away
things. We use them to look back in time
and understand how the universe formed.
We use them to see distant planets, where
other people might live. We use them to
gather invisible light, to see things no one
has ever seen before.

Some animals, like the aye-aye,
have very large eyes, to help them
see in the dark. You are using
your eyes right now, to look at this
picture of an aye-aye's eyes.

LENSES

If you look at a flame or a light bulb or a firefly or the Sun
or a star you are seeing a light source, a thing that creates light.

When you see an object, light
that last touched that object has
bounced into your eyeball. Inside
your eyeball is a lens that bends
light onto the back of your eye.

Lenses are clear curved
shapes that gather, bend,
and concentrate light.

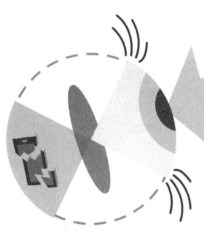

When a lens gathers, bends, and
concentrates light on a particular
place, this is called focusing.

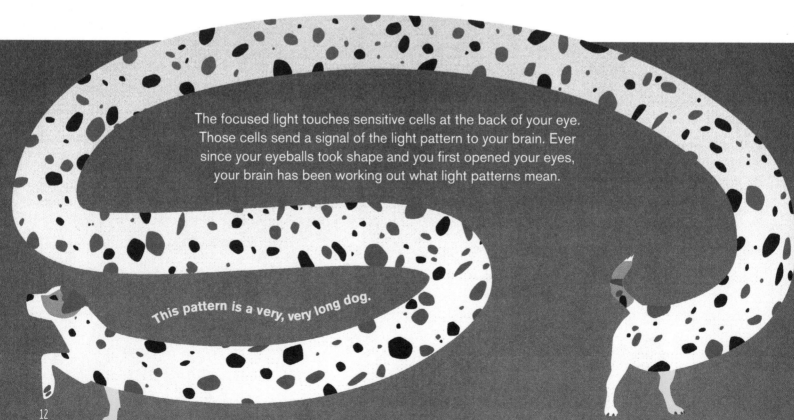

The focused light touches sensitive cells at the back of your eye.
Those cells send a signal of the light pattern to your brain. Ever
since your eyeballs took shape and you first opened your eyes,
your brain has been working out what light patterns mean.

This pattern is a very, very long dog.

Some human eyes can see faraway mountains and all the colors on this page. But sometimes people want to look at things that are farther than mountains, and see more colors than human eyes can see.

For over four hundred years, people have built telescopes to see farther and farther, in more and more colors.

THE FIRST TELESCOPE

Galileo Galilei was born over 450 years ago in Italy. He was curious about how things moved, how they looked, and what they were made of. When he learned an eyeglass-maker in the Netherlands had built a tube with lenses that made faraway things appear closer, he was intrigued. He learned how this spyglass worked, and built a larger one for himself.

Galileo's telescope made things appear 33 times closer. If he looked through the lenses at something 33 yards away, it would look as if it was right in front of him. Nobody had ever improved their sight in this way before!

When he pointed his telescope at the night sky, Galileo saw amazing things: valleys, craters, and mountains on the Moon. Later, he looked at the planets, and was able to see moons orbiting Jupiter.

He showed how the changing appearance and position of the planets can be explained by the Earth and other planets all revolving around the Sun. This was controversial at the time, but now everyone knows it to be true.

NEAR AND FAR, DIM AND BRIGHT

On a summer night, fireflies blink on and off with greenish light. Even though they are small and dim, because they are so close, we can see them and they can see each other.

If you look up at the stars, some of them might be about as bright as a firefly. It might be fun to think that they are so small and near that you could grab them and put them in a jar.

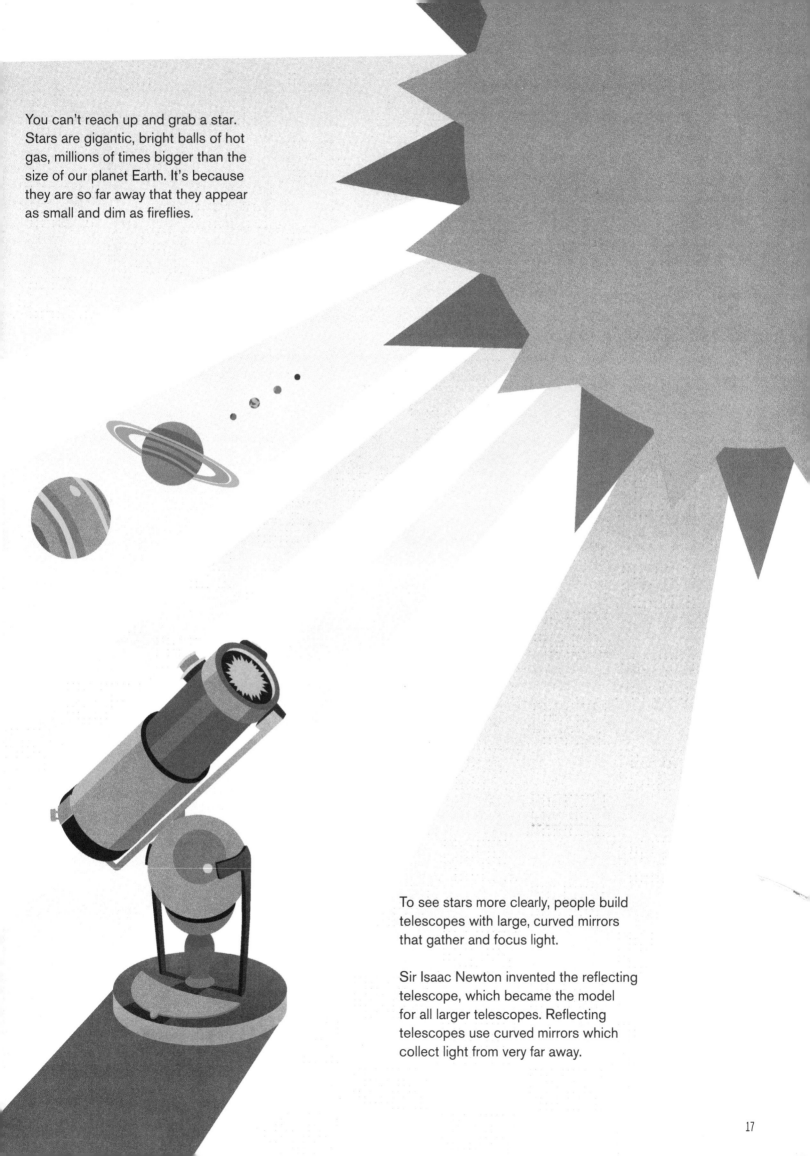

You can't reach up and grab a star. Stars are gigantic, bright balls of hot gas, millions of times bigger than the size of our planet Earth. It's because they are so far away that they appear as small and dim as fireflies.

To see stars more clearly, people build telescopes with large, curved mirrors that gather and focus light.

Sir Isaac Newton invented the reflecting telescope, which became the model for all larger telescopes. Reflecting telescopes use curved mirrors which collect light from very far away.

REFLECTING AND COLLECTING

The deep mirrors in telescopes are like baskets or bowls. They collect light from distant stars, like buckets collecting raindrops.

Mirrors come in different shapes for different purposes. Flat mirrors are good to see what you look like when you are brushing your teeth. Bulging mirrors are good to see the cars behind you.

Light does not pool in the bottom of a mirror like water in the bottom of a bucket. When light touches a mirror, it bounces off again. This is called reflecting. Curved telescope mirrors reflect the collected light to a focal point.

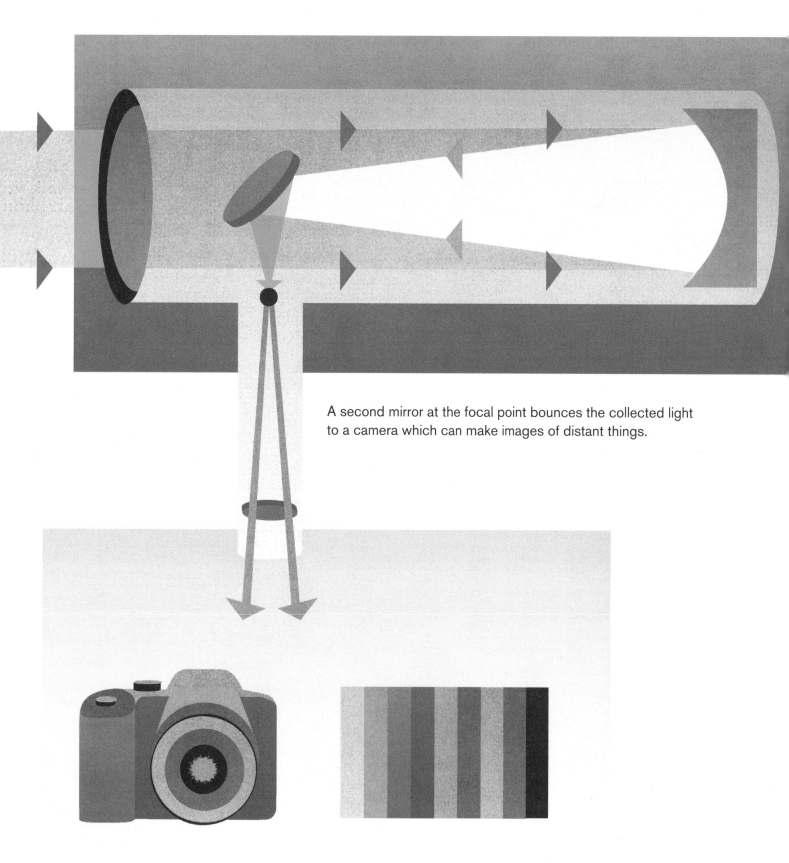

A second mirror at the focal point bounces the collected light to a camera which can make images of distant things.

THE KECK OBSERVATORY

In the middle of the ocean is an island called Hawai'i.
In the middle of Hawai'i is a mountain called Maunakea.
At the top of Maunakea, there are many observatories,
including the Keck Observatory.

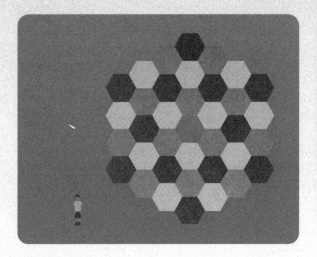

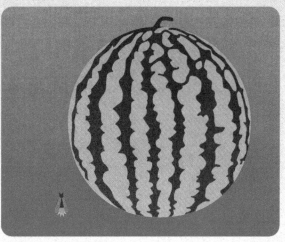

This huge observatory has two enormous telescopes. The 11-yard mirrors are made of 36 segments. Together, they can gather 80 million times more light than the lens of a human eyeball.

Standing next to the 11-yard mirror, you would feel like a firefly beside a watermelon.

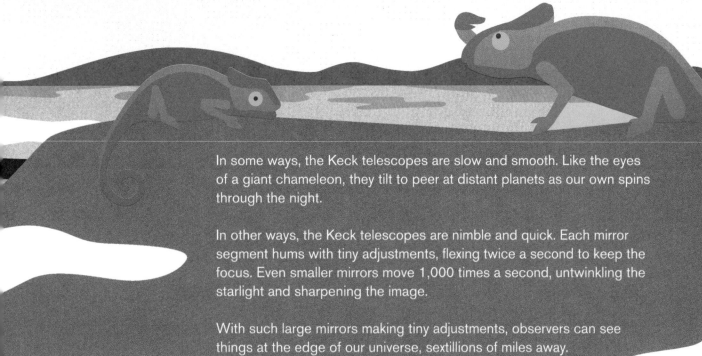

In some ways, the Keck telescopes are slow and smooth. Like the eyes of a giant chameleon, they tilt to peer at distant planets as our own spins through the night.

In other ways, the Keck telescopes are nimble and quick. Each mirror segment hums with tiny adjustments, flexing twice a second to keep the focus. Even smaller mirrors move 1,000 times a second, untwinkling the starlight and sharpening the image.

With such large mirrors making tiny adjustments, observers can see things at the edge of our universe, sextillions of miles away.

LARGE DISTANCES

One way to talk about a distance is how long it takes to get there.

Your eyeball is 94 million miles from the Sun. The Sun is very large and very far away but sunlight only takes eight minutes and twenty seconds to reach your eyeball. That is because light moves very fast. In fact, light is the fastest thing in the universe.

The sunshine touching your eyeball left the Sun eight minutes and twenty seconds ago. Other stars are so far away it takes years for their light to reach our eyes. Some light travels for billions of years.

A light year is the distance light travels in a year: about 5.8 trillion miles. If you look up at the star Proxima Centauri today, you'll see the light that left four years ago, when you and the star were four years younger. That star, our nearest neighbor after the Sun, is four light years away.

When we see old starlight, we are looking back in time. The deeper we look into space, the more we can learn about the shapes of things long ago, when the universe was just beginning.

INVISIBLE COLORS

There are types of light we can see and types we can't. The visible parts of light are made up of all the colors that the human eye can detect. The parts of the spectrum outside of the visible range are called the infrared and ultraviolet spectrum. These invisible lights include X-rays and gamma rays.

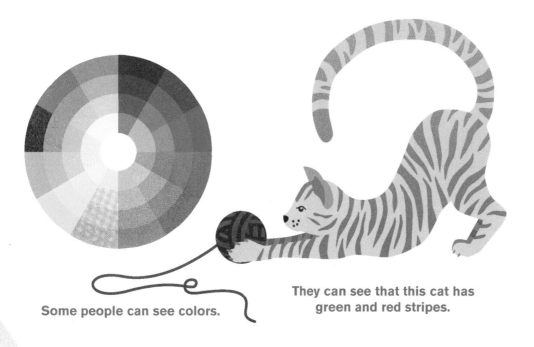

Some people can see colors.

They can see that this cat has green and red stripes.

They can see that this cheeseburger is blue.

Sunburns are caused by ultraviolet light. Even more compact and energetic invisible purples are called X-rays and gamma rays. They are so compact and energetic they can pass right through your body. Too much exposure to X-rays and gamma rays can damage living things and cause cancer.

People build telescopes of different shapes to gather different colors of invisible light. Just like there are particular spots that are good to gather different fruits, there are particular places on Earth and in space that are good for gathering different colors of invisible light.

Using a prism, we can see sunlight split into a rainbow of different colors.

People who can't see colors are sometimes called "color-blind."

In a sense, we are all color-blind, because there are so many colors we cannot see with our human eyes.

Snakes can sense light that is redder than our reddest red. When light is very red, it has a long shape. We call it infrared. The longer its shape, the more spread out its energy. When light is longer than infrared, we call it microwave or radio wave.

On the other side of the rainbow, bees can see light more purple than our purplest purple. When light is purple, its wavelength is short and compact. The more compact its shape, the more densely packed its energy. Invisible purple lights buzz with so much energy that it can actually hurt us.

VISTA

On a mountaintop in Chile, in the high desert above the clouds, the VISTA telescope gathers invisible red light from the center of the galaxy.

VISTA's mirror was designed in England, made in Germany, polished in Russia, and installed in Chile. Working together, people from across our world created this useful instrument to help us understand how stars begin.

On a clear night, you might see the Milky Way overhead. Many people have looked up and wondered what it is. Some call it by different names: The Bird's Way, the Silver River, or The Way the Dog Ran Away. When we look into that glowing stripe, we are looking into the busiest part of our own galaxy, which is shaped like a spiral. The glow is the blended light from hundreds of billions of distant stars, gas and dust.

They are not alive but, like living things, stars change over time. They form from clouds of gas, shine for a few billion years, and then either cool down or explode. When a star stops shining, it leaves behind clouds of dust and ice floating in space. Looking into the Milky Way is like looking through a thick cloud of dust. The dust blocks visible light that human eyes can see. But invisible red light slips through this interstellar dust, like a snake between rocks. Using special telescopes, we can collect this infrared light and understand what is happening beyond the dust, within our own galaxy.

Observers use the VISTA telescope to see glowing clouds of hydrogen gas. As clouds clump closer and closer, they warm, glowing with infrared light that VISTA can detect. Some clumps get so large and hot and bright they become stars. These distant gas clouds are called stellar nurseries—the place where stars are born.

JAMES WEBB SPACE TELESCOPE

Space is a good place for a telescope. In space, there is no atmosphere to bump, bend, or scramble the light. Space is also extremely cold, which is good for the sensors that detect invisible infrared light.

The James Webb Space Telescope is designed to be folded into a capsule and launched into space with a rocket. After three days of flying, it will emerge like a butterfly from a chrysalis, unfurling a shield to protect it from the Sun's heat. Seven days later, 18 golden mirrors will open to collect invisible infrared starlight. After 14 days, the James Webb Space Telescope will sit beyond the Moon, nearly 1 million miles from Earth.

The James Webb Space Telescope will face away from the Sun, looking out into the Milky Way for planets around other stars. Astronomers think that almost every star has planets.

Some of these planets are made of the same stuff that the Earth is made of, including rocks and water. People might live on those planets. Maybe they are looking up at the sky or reading a book like this one.

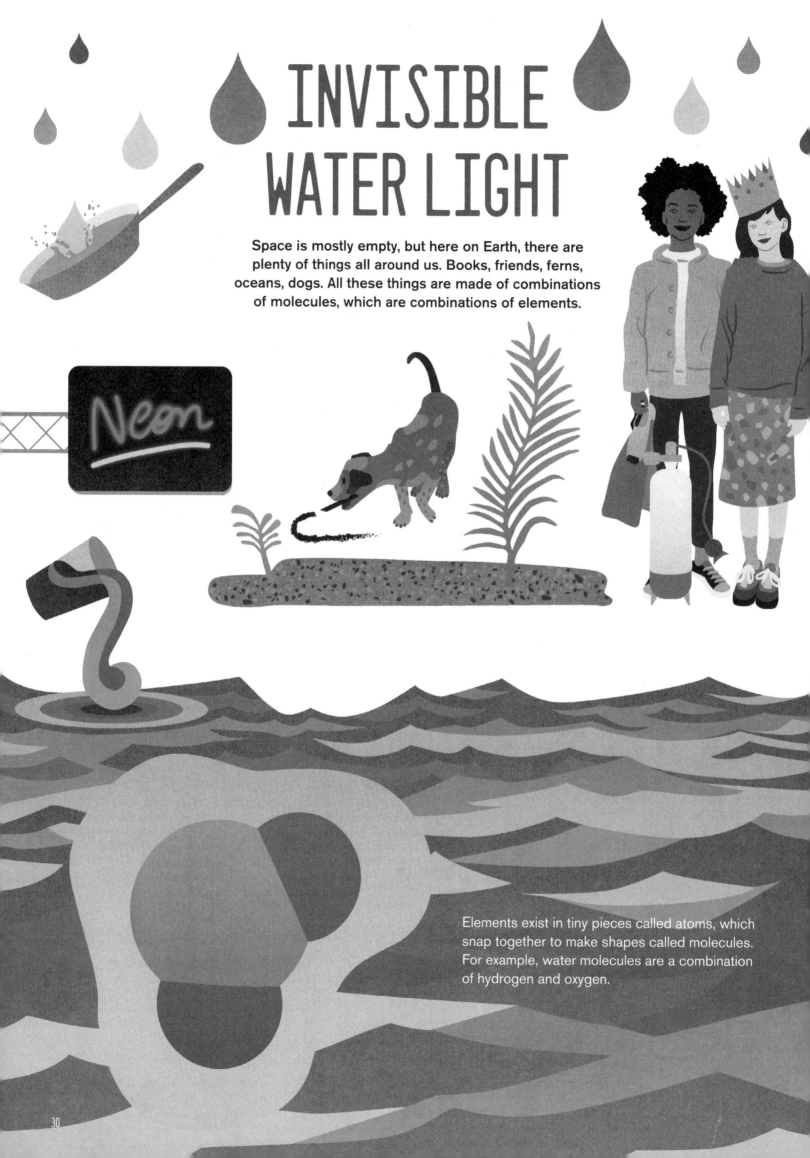

INVISIBLE WATER LIGHT

Space is mostly empty, but here on Earth, there are plenty of things all around us. Books, friends, ferns, oceans, dogs. All these things are made of combinations of molecules, which are combinations of elements.

Neon

Elements exist in tiny pieces called atoms, which snap together to make shapes called molecules. For example, water molecules are a combination of hydrogen and oxygen.

All living things need water.
People who are interested in finding signs of life search for signs of water.

Every element and molecule can create and absorb particular colors of light. When water molecules jostle each other in space, they send out invisible light redder than infrared. This invisible water light is called millimeter radiation.

Whenever a certain type of atom or molecule emits a certain color of light, other atoms or molecules of the same shape can absorb that color. If water in one part of the galaxy makes millimeter radiation, another water molecule on Earth can drink it right up. The air we breathe, our atmosphere, is full of water vapor.

For this reason, when people look for water in outer space, they place millimeter telescopes in the driest deserts high above the clouds, where there is less water to interfere.

ALMA

High in the Atacama Desert in South America, in one of the driest places in the world, a giant observatory gathers invisible light from distant molecules. A group of telescopes is called an array. The Atacama Large Millimeter Array has sixty-six 13-yard dishes that work together. Each dish is about half the size of a basketball court.

These dishes are smooth, but not shiny. The millimeter light they collect does not need a mirror to be focused. The curved shape of the surface focuses invisible light onto detectors. The information from the 66 detectors is combined by computers, which make visible images from invisible light.

Fifty of the giant dishes are on wheels. When observers want to look at a large area of the sky, they drive the dishes apart. When they want to record from a tiny patch of sky, they drive the dishes closer together. This is like zooming in and out with a camera.

Using ALMA, observers have found discs of snow swirling around distant stars. This is the same kind of snow you might play with in the winter. Over time, the snow may clump together with elements and molecules to form a planet. Perhaps other children might play there in the snow someday.

RADIO LIGHT

Long, invisible light waves are often called radio waves.
Radio light moves freely through the atmosphere. Water does not
block it. Cell phones and car stereos can translate radio light into sounds.

Because so many people communicate using cell phones,
it can be hard to tell which radio signals come from people
and which ones come from the sky. For this reason, radio
telescopes work best far from cities.

Radio telescopes translate radio light into pictures. Radio light can be collected from sources in outer space, like spinning quasars and pulsars, and even whole galaxies. We also listen for signals from other planets.

35

GIANT DISHES

On the Caribbean island of Puerto Rico, in the middle of the jungle, is the Arecibo Radio Telescope. It is about 1,000 feet across, with a 5 million square foot surface. You could fit a town in that amount of space! The giant dish is fixed in place, but the 900-ton dome suspended above it can be moved to change the focus of radio light.

In China, in the mountains of Guizhou province, people built the Five-hundred meter Aperture Spherical Telescope, called FAST. It is even larger than Arecibo. The FAST dish is built from thousands of triangular panels that can be adjusted to focus the radio light. People can use large dishes like Arecibo and FAST to send radio signals into space.

Scientists have sent out messages about who we are, such as the Arecibo message (left). Perhaps people on other planets will receive these messages with their own radio telescopes and send messages back to us.

37

STRETCHED COLORS

When something makes light, the color of that light carries information. By understanding color, observers can understand the temperature of the light source, what it is made of, and in which direction it is moving.

Some light is red to begin with, like the red light from a neon sign.

Other light starts out green, like the light from a firefly. . .

. . . or blue, like the light from a gas stove.

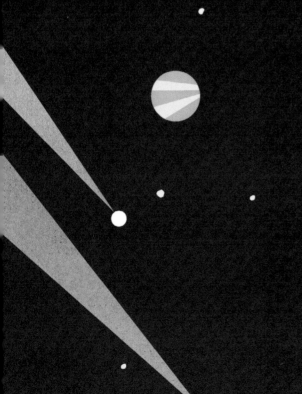

Light can start as one color, but change into a different color if the light source is moving. As the light source moves away from an observer, its color becomes a little redder. The light is stretched over long distances. Sometimes visible light gets stretched so much it becomes invisible infrared, or even radio light.

Astronomers call this color change a redshift.

Everything in the universe is moving. Just as fireflies move through moonlight, moons move around planets, planets move around stars, and stars move around galaxies. Most galaxies are moving away from each other. When a star or galaxy looks redder than an observer expects, that means it is moving away very quickly.

If someone in a distant galaxy used a telescope to see our yellow Sun, it would look red to them. If their telescope could see a firefly blinking, that firefly would blink red instead of green.

A HUM IN A HORN

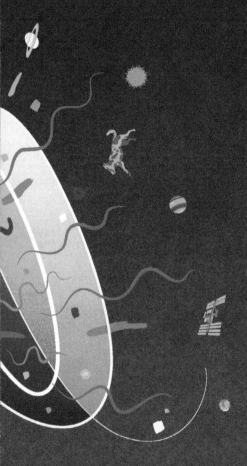

In 1964, people from Bell Labs in America were using a horn-shaped telescope to look for radio signals from space.

Observers rotated the horn, collecting radio waves from all over the sky. All around, in every direction, they found a particular color of radio light. No matter where they pointed the horn, they found the same (invisible) color, fuzzing and hissing.

At first, they thought the problem was that pigeons were living in the horn. They cleaned out the pigeon nests, but still found the same radio light wherever they looked. Talking with other astronomers, they learned that these radio waves were stretched out light from very early times in the universe. In fact, what they were hearing were radio echoes of the first moments of the universe.

Billions of years ago, every place and all the stuff that would become everything we know and see—all the stars, planets, galaxies, dogs, clouds, and comets—were packed into a very tiny area. Then, at some moment, maybe the first moment, everything spread out very fast and was extremely hot. We call this moment the "Big Bang."

A few hundred thousand years later, electrons and protons began to cool down and fuse into hydrogen atoms. As they formed atoms, they emitted light, and the expanding universe began to glow. Since then, everything has continued to fly away, faster and faster, expanding in every direction. Over billions of years, that first hydrogen glow has stretched redder and redder, from visible, to infrared, to microwave and radio light that can be detected using radio telescopes.

THE LONGEST LIGHT FROM LONG AGO

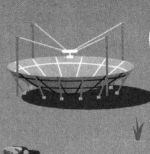

In Australia, in the Western Desert, thousands of antennas poke up from the ground like metal whiskers. Long radio light waves—as long as an elephant's trunk, as looong as a fire hose, as loooooong as a train twisting through a tunnel— tickle these whiskers in different patterns.

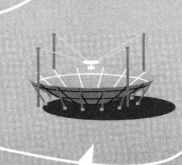

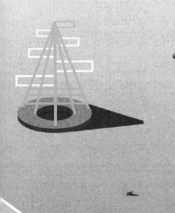

Low Frequency Aperture Array, Australia

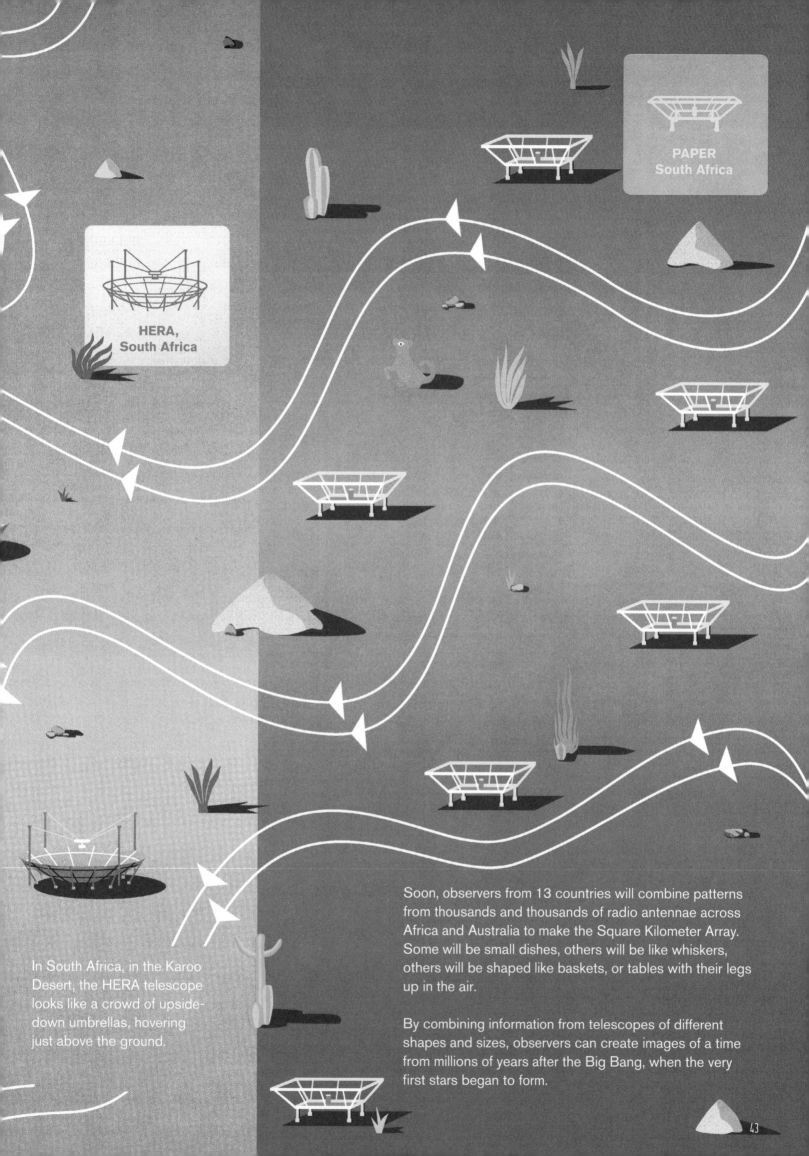

HERA,
South Africa

PAPER
South Africa

In South Africa, in the Karoo Desert, the HERA telescope looks like a crowd of upside-down umbrellas, hovering just above the ground.

Soon, observers from 13 countries will combine patterns from thousands and thousands of radio antennae across Africa and Australia to make the Square Kilometer Array. Some will be small dishes, others will be like whiskers, others will be shaped like baskets, or tables with their legs up in the air.

By combining information from telescopes of different shapes and sizes, observers can create images of a time from millions of years after the Big Bang, when the very first stars began to form.

43

A PICTURE
OF NOTHING

For many years, astronomers had predicted
black holes, but nobody had ever gathered
light to make an image of one. A black hole
is a point in space that has gravity so strong
that nothing can escape it.

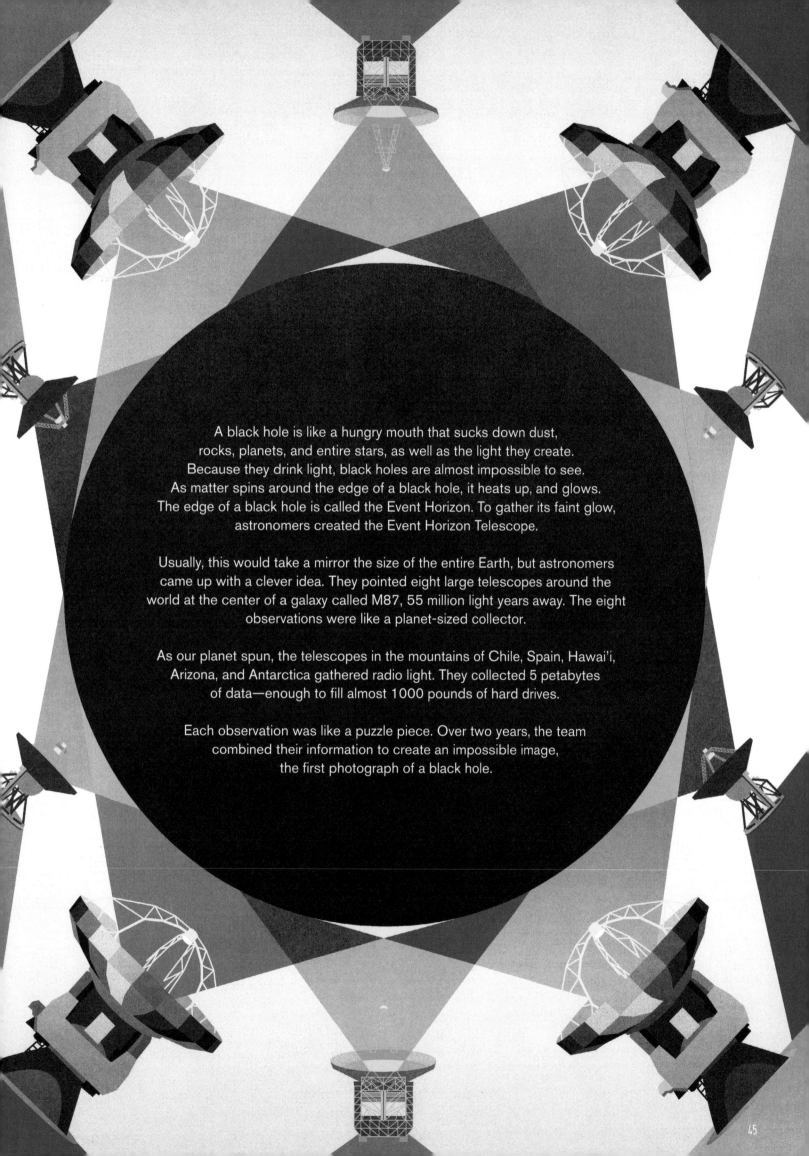

A black hole is like a hungry mouth that sucks down dust,
rocks, planets, and entire stars, as well as the light they create.
Because they drink light, black holes are almost impossible to see.
As matter spins around the edge of a black hole, it heats up, and glows.
The edge of a black hole is called the Event Horizon. To gather its faint glow,
astronomers created the Event Horizon Telescope.

Usually, this would take a mirror the size of the entire Earth, but astronomers
came up with a clever idea. They pointed eight large telescopes around the
world at the center of a galaxy called M87, 55 million light years away. The eight
observations were like a planet-sized collector.

As our planet spun, the telescopes in the mountains of Chile, Spain, Hawai'i,
Arizona, and Antarctica gathered radio light. They collected 5 petabytes
of data—enough to fill almost 1000 pounds of hard drives.

Each observation was like a puzzle piece. Over two years, the team
combined their information to create an impossible image,
the first photograph of a black hole.

HUBBLE SPACE TELESCOPE

Just like there are invisible red lights, on the other side of the visible rainbow are invisible purples, called ultraviolet, or UV. The hottest parts of our Sun make UV light, but most of it is scattered by our atmosphere. For this reason, astronomers launch telescopes into space to collect it.

The Hubble space telescope captures infrared light, visible colors and UV light. Hubble's mirror is a curved and polished dish, like the ones at the Keck observatory.

Hubble has collected light from young stars that burn so hot they shine with UV light, unlike the visible light of our yellow Sun. By studying the images, people hope to understand why these young stars often form in clusters.

Observers have used the Hubble space telescope to detect liquid water on Ganymede, one of Jupiter's moons. Ganymede emits an invisible ultraviolet glow that bends as it goes around Jupiter. Observers think the bending is caused by an ocean of water sloshing beneath miles of ice on Ganymede's surface.

X-RAY EYES

When elements are heated to temperatures even hotter than our Sun, they shine with light that buzzes so fast that curved lenses and mirrors can't focus it.

This kind of invisible light is called X-rays. X-rays are blocked by the atmosphere, so X-ray telescopes must be in space in order to collect them.

To gather X-rays from distant sources and focus them to make images, people build nested mirrors. X-rays enter a nest of golden mirrors and buzz back and forth between them, like bees trapped between window panes. The trapped X-rays are guided into a detector that creates an image.

One telescope with this kind of X-ray trap is the Chandra Space Telescope. It can find objects hotter than the hottest star, like gas clouds falling into black holes and entire galaxies crashing into each other, buzzing with invisible light.

GAMMA RAY EYES

Gamma rays are even more purple than X-rays. They are created when stars collapse in upon themselves and explode in a massive burst of heat and light. Gamma rays have so much energy that they can pass through a mirror without bouncing off.

When Gamma rays pass through things, sometimes they crash into the center of an atom. When this happens, the atom sheds a couple of tiny pieces. Those pieces bump into other atoms, which then bump into other atoms. Each bump releases a bit of light that we can detect.

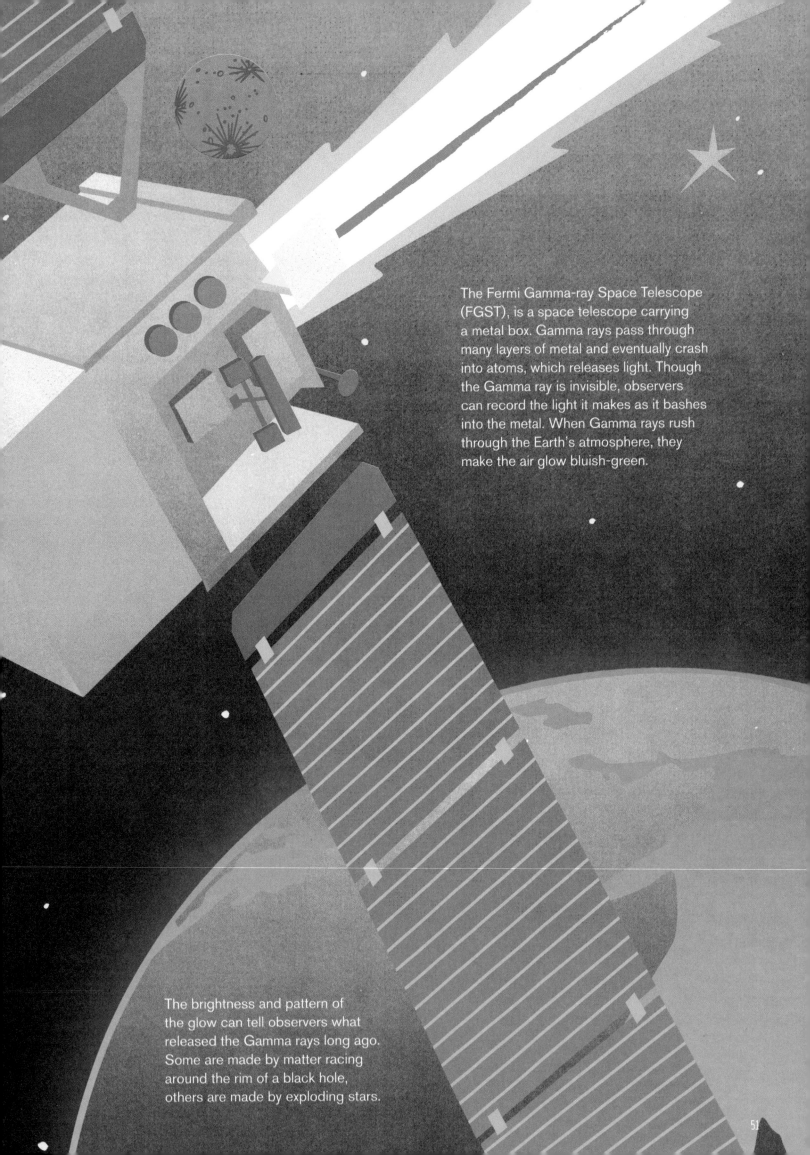

The Fermi Gamma-ray Space Telescope (FGST), is a space telescope carrying a metal box. Gamma rays pass through many layers of metal and eventually crash into atoms, which releases light. Though the Gamma ray is invisible, observers can record the light it makes as it bashes into the metal. When Gamma rays rush through the Earth's atmosphere, they make the air glow bluish-green.

The brightness and pattern of the glow can tell observers what released the Gamma rays long ago. Some are made by matter racing around the rim of a black hole, others are made by exploding stars.

LITTLE EYES

There are millions of people all over the world with small telescopes. They go out on dark nights to look at the sky. Sometimes they might see something that big telescopes miss. They might find a star that wasn't there before, or a dim star exploding in a supernova.

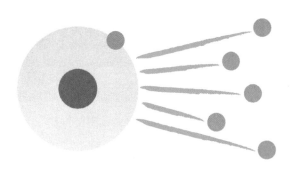

Supernovas

All stars start as collections of hydrogen and helium gas. As gravity draws the gas together, the hydrogen fuses, releasing light and heat and creating other elements like carbon, nitrogen, and silicon. The energy from the fusion at the center presses outward, keeping the star spherical, but when it runs out of hydrogen to fuse, gravity draws the star in on itself. When everything falls into the center, it becomes extremely hot, and blows apart in a super-energetic explosion called a supernova.

A supernova can shine brighter than an entire galaxy for a few weeks, scattering elements into clouds of dust that float through space. When someone with a small telescope sees a supernova, they contact observers at the big telescopes who focus on the event. By gathering light from exploding stars, we can understand how the elements that make our world are forged.